AN INVITATION FROM GOD

STEVE JENNERICH

CONTENTS

Acknowledgments	v
Introduction	vii
1. Don't Be Intimidated	1
2. Eternity	9
3. What About My Past?	15
4. What Will People Think?	20
5. Run Your Race	26
6. What Is Faith?	32
7. Will I Still Have Struggles?	37
8. Make God Your Bff	43
9. Who Am I Now?	50
10. God's Not Done With You	56
11. What Now?	63
12. Life's Worth Living	69
Afterword	73
Also by Steve Jennerich	75
Notes	77

An Invitation from God: A Lighthearted Introduction to Getting to Know God from a Lifetime Blue Collar Guy!

By Steve Jennerich

© 2023 Steve Jennerich

All rights reserved. Printed in the United States of America. No part of this publication may be reproduced, stored in a retrieval system or transmitted in any form or by any means, electronic, mechanical, photocopying, recording or otherwise, without the written permission of the publisher.

Scriptures taken from the Holy Bible, New International Version®, NIV®. Copyright © 1973, 1978, 1984, 2011 by Biblica, Inc.™ Used by permission of Zondervan. All rights reserved worldwide. www.zondervan.com. The "NIV" and "New International Version" are trademarks registered in the United States Patent and Trademark Office by Biblica, Inc.™

❦ Created with Vellum

ACKNOWLEDGMENTS

There are several people I would like to dedicate this book to. First and foremost, I give all the honor and glory and credit to God. Without Him, there would be no me. So thank you, God, for inspiring me to be better and not to give up.

Thank you to my two incredible kids, Alex and Madison. You have turned into the most incredible young adults that any dad could ask for. Thanks for being strong and for never giving up on me. I love you both so much. You are my life.

Thank you to my four brothers; Bob, Mike, Doug, and Tom. You guys have always been there for me, and I greatly appreciate that. Love you all.

I love all my brothers the same, but I need to give special thanks to Pastor Bob, also known as my older brother. I could not have done this without you. Words cannot describe what your mentorship and friendship have done for me. I am eternally grateful.

Mom and Dad, thank you so much for being the best parents that anyone could ask for. You have always been there for me, and I don't know what I would do without you. You are great examples and have supported me through everything in life. You are my true heroes, and I love you both so much!

INTRODUCTION

I don't know about you, but prior to accepting Jesus, the idea of becoming a Christian and having a personal relationship with God seemed so mysterious and confusing to me. Quite honestly, I didn't even really know what that meant. How can you have a personal relationship with someone you can't even see or touch or hear? I found it very strange when I would hear people say they had a personal relationship with God. I would just think, "Yeah, sure you do. What have you been smoking?" That kind of talk just made me uncomfortable. I always "believed in God." I believed God was up there in heaven somewhere. But I was far from having a personal relationship with Him or even knowing how to start the communication process. As crazy as it seemed to me though, if such a relationship was possible, I wanted it. I just had no idea how to make this happen. Years later, I came to find that it absolutely is possible and how simple it really is.

Naturally, before you experience this personal relationship, all kinds of thoughts and questions might run through your mind. You may have many misconceptions about the process of having a relationship with God. Will I have to study something and take a test? Do I need to be voted into this "club"? Is there some sort of initiation? Will there be a ceremony? If I go through with this, will I have to go knocking on doors telling people about this? Do I need to buy incense to burn in my house? Can I still hang out with my friends who aren't Christians? While we're on that topic, what will my friends and family and coworkers think? What if I've never really been a church person and I'm not even sure how to pray properly? What if I've done some really bad things in my past? Relax! We all have! That's what makes us human!

Besides all these questions and concerns, I also wasn't sure if I "qualified," so to speak. I am a lifetime blue collar guy. I was a wrestler in high school. I never worked in an office in my life. At eleven years old, I had my own lawn mowing business. My dad would drive me to my customers' houses with the lawn mower in the station wagon, and I would do my jobs. Throughout high school, in between school and sports, I worked at a gas station part-time and full-time during the summer as well. After high school I went to college for one year

INTRODUCTION

and decided I wasn't cut out for that. From there I went to work at an auto repair garage. Over the years, I also did some bartending and construction work. Why do I share this with you? My entire working career of over thirty-five years has been spent at auto repair garages, construction sites, and bars. Not exactly the places you would think of to look for God. But that didn't matter. God found me and never let me go, and I have never let Him go either. I have since developed an incredible relationship with God. Transparently speaking, one that I never would have thought was possible. Thankfully God doesn't care about your background and couldn't care less what color your collar is. God cares about the color of your heart and that's it. By the way, Jesus was a blue collar man Himself before He began His ministry, so I felt like I was in good company.

As silly as some of those questions and thoughts above may seem, they stop many people from taking that first step. When I say step, I mean any personal steps and decisions in your life that bring you closer to God. No one gets a list of instructions to follow in order to have a relationship with God. If somebody does give you a list of dos and don'ts, *run*! In fact, becoming a Christian and having a personal relationship with God is only between you and God. That's it! No test, no voting, no initiation, no knocking on doors, no incense, and no ceremony (sorry about the ceremony part if you were looking to be celebrated. You may not be celebrated here on Earth, but you will be in heaven). Now, if you truly desire to have this relationship, it would be a good idea to start studying the Bible and to surround yourself with Christians to help you with your journey. But again, nobody has any "say" in your relationship with God except you and God. Isn't that cool?

It is my heartfelt passion to be able to help you in having that relationship. I want to walk you through the simplicity of knowing the Creator of the universe (and the Creator of you) on a personal level. I would also like to clear up some potentially negative preconceived notions you may have in order to put you at ease. I want to let you know that I know exactly how you feel. I had hit rock bottom in my life and didn't know where to turn. If it wasn't for reaching to God for help, and Him reaching back, it scares me to think about where I would be right now. Your life will change dramatically for the better too.

Here's the best part: I will cover this more later, but your past doesn't matter. You could have a little faith, a lot of faith, or no faith at all. What's important is who your faith is in. No matter who you are or where you've been, your exciting new life begins today. I am so proud of you for wanting to enhance this area of your life. I thank you for allowing me to walk you through it. I will promise you this: there is no more important area of your life to enhance than your relationship with God. And regardless of who you are or where you've been,

INTRODUCTION

God wants to be involved in every area of your life. Get excited to know that God wants a relationship with you even more than you want one with Him. I hate for this to sound like a slogan, but here it is: Give God a chance! You won't regret it!

CHAPTER 1
DON'T BE INTIMIDATED

I'M NOT GONNA LIE. I used to be intimidated by certain words and phrases that Christians used. I would like to put your mind at ease by clearing some of this up right away. First of all, what does it mean or what does it take to be a Christian? In its simplest terms, being a Christian means believing in Jesus Christ and choosing to follow Him. If that wasn't easy enough, I'd like to ease your mind even further. One great misconception people have is that being a Christian means following all kinds of rules and regulations and doing certain rituals. It's not that at all. It's not even about going to church. It simply means developing a "friendship" with Jesus Christ. And that is just between you and Him. You can breathe now!

Maybe you already have a little bit of faith, but don't know where to go from here. Perhaps you grew up like

I did, and you just went to church because your parents made you. I am the second of five boys. There were times my parents would go to church on Saturday night. My brothers and I didn't want to go then, so we were supposed to go on Sunday morning. Most of the time we would just hang out and go to the candy store and show up to the church right before it ended so we could grab the weekly bulletin to bring home to prove we were at church. (I know! I know! Don't judge me! I was young and God still loves me.) My mom would ask me, "What was the message about in church today?" And I would say "God." She was on to me! The fact is, many people only go to church to avoid feelings of guilt or because they feel obligated to God, or to somebody else, to do so. Those are bad reasons. There is absolutely nothing wrong with going to church. I highly recommend it. But you need to find the right church, and you need to be going for the right reasons. Whether you are just beginning your faith journey or you would like to renew your faith, I will show you how easy and rewarding this will be.

There is a massive difference between religion and relationship. I have an incredible relationship with God —a relationship I never thought I could have—and yet it grows stronger every day. Having said that, I am not so-called religious. Being religious often means following rules and rituals. Some of them teach that your salvation is works-based, meaning you have to do certain deeds to earn your way into heaven. That couldn't be further from the truth. You *cannot* earn your way into heaven. All the good deeds in the world aren't going to get you there. There's nothing wrong with doing those good deeds, but that's not the answer. You will not be "saved" by your works, but only by God's grace. Jesus paid the ultimate price to save you. He died for you. And here's all you need to do. Are you ready? You need to believe that Jesus died for your sins and that He rose from the dead. You need to believe that Jesus is who He says He is. You need to have a desire to turn away from sin and a desire to turn to God. That's it. It's that simple. That doesn't mean you won't sin. We all sin every day. But when you develop a relationship with Jesus, you develop a heartfelt desire to not *want* to sin anymore.

You can literally turn your entire life around by saying a prayer as simple as this:

God, I come to you because I want a relationship with you. I believe that you sent your Son, Jesus, to die for my sins. I believe He rose from the dead and is in heaven with you right now. Please forgive me for my sins. Please come into my heart. I would like to accept your Son, Jesus Christ, as my Lord and Savior. Please guide me from here into your purposes for my life.

If you prayed that prayer, can you believe that you just changed your entire future, both here and in heaven, by simply praying that prayer? How can it be that simple? It's simple because Jesus did all the work. All He asks of you is to believe it from your heart. As simple as it is, though, it's the biggest decision you will ever make in your life. If you prayed that prayer, Congratulations!!! You are now a Christian. Welcome to the "club."

I will now tell you about the words and phrases that scared me or turned me off. They scared me because I didn't really know what they meant. I didn't like to hear about eternity. I didn't like to hear about heaven and hell. It creeped me out to hear somebody say they were "saved." And it made my skin crawl to hear somebody say they were "born again." When I heard somebody say they were a born-again Christian, my only thought was, *Uh oh, duck, you're about to get hit in the head with a Bible*. God forgive me, but I used to look at these people as religious freaks. Their words and phrases terrified me. You know why? Because I did not educate myself on their true meaning. Can you believe that just by saying that simple prayer, you are both saved and born again? Let me explain before you get scared. When you were born into this world, you automatically became part of your family here on Earth. You were born to your mom and dad. When you make the decision to be part of God's family, and pray a prayer like the one above, you are now born again—born into God's family by choice. A choice that only you can make. Being born again simply means to establish a relationship with God. And being "saved" simply means the same thing: because you have that relationship, you are now saved by God's grace and will spend eternity with Him in heaven and not in hell. Yeah, forgive me for slipping that word in there, but it's the truth. Once you pass on from this world to the next, you will spend eternity somewhere (more on this in the next chapter). The great news is, it's your choice where you spend it. Doesn't that make you feel better?

And no, this doesn't mean you have to run around announcing to the world that you are a born-again Christian and that you are saved by God's grace and that you are going to heaven, not hell. Can you imagine if I had done that at the auto repair garage or the construction sites where I worked? I would have gotten a pipe wrench thrown at me. Don't get me wrong. I have absolutely no shame in being a Christian. In fact, I'm very proud of it. However, there's a right way and a wrong way to do things. You want to attract people so you have the chance to share the good news with them when the time is right. Trust me, people will start to notice a change in you, and they will be asking you what's changed. They will want to know what you know. That's when you have the opportunity to share what you've learned and to offer them the same opportunity. You can now share with them that it's not *what* you know but *who* you know. And you don't have to tell anybody if you don't want to. However, as this relationship grows stronger, you will probably feel inclined to share it with other people. That's great. But it's also your choice who to share it with and when to share it with them.

Let me throw one more term at you before we move on: God-fearing! Woah, that one scared me. Why do I need to be afraid of God? I thought God loved me. You don't need to be afraid of God, and He absolutely loves you. That's not what God-fearing means. The word *fear* here means a reverential fear, which really means to be in total awe and amazement of how grand God is, having absolute respect and appreciation for the greatness of God and what He has done for you. When you begin this relationship with God, He will come into your heart and start to work on you. He will help you with wanting not to sin and leading a better life. Once I learned the true meaning of *God-fearing*, my only fear was letting God down. Fear of disappointing Him. Fear of not allowing Him to go work in my life, blocking Him from helping me become everything that He created me to be. Fear of not making Him proud of me. This is the only fear I have now when it comes to God. Not fear of what He will do to me when I sin. God will allow certain things to happen in your life to keep you on track, but we are all sinners. If we weren't, Jesus would not have needed to die for us.

At this point, you may be thinking, *Well, if Jesus died for my sins and I can't earn my way into heaven, then I can just say that prayer and do whatever I want and God will forgive me and one day I'll be in heaven*. Sorry to burst your bubble, but it doesn't work that way. Remember when I told you that you have to believe from your heart? Once you say it and truly mean it, that's when God will start working on your heart and you will feel it. You will not want to continue the same sinful behavior that you have in the past. Let me reiterate. You will still be a sinner. You will still sin. Jesus is the only sinless person who will ever walk this earth. But your desire not to sin gets stronger and stronger because you have now started to develop a relationship with the true person of God. Just like you would not want to let anybody in your family down, the people you love the most, this is how you start to feel about God. Be patient. This all takes time. But it's worth it.

I'm not insulting myself or claiming to be stupid by any means, but I think that because of my blue-collar background, I wanted things explained to me as simply as possible. Especially in this area. I can't tell you how excited I was when I found out how simple having a relationship with God is. I keep using the word *simple* because there really is so little to it. It *is* simple. But it's not easy. You are going to need to change some things that you are currently doing, and you will want to learn more about God and what He wants from your relationship. But if you didn't want that change, you probably wouldn't be reading this right now. I am not a pastor, nor did I go to seminary. Thankfully, neither is necessary to have an incredible personal relationship with God. I am just a regular, everyday guy who learned that God, the Creator of the universe, wanted to be my friend. I get goose bumps just thinking about that. It doesn't matter who you are, or where you've been, or what you've done. None of that matters. As soon as you make that decision, God erases all of that from His memory and your new life begins immediately. I hope you're as excited about that as I was.

CHAPTER 2
ETERNITY

WHY DOES it frighten us to talk about eternity? The obvious reason is because it is associated with dying. I'm with you. Who wants to talk about dying? However, dying is one of the only guarantees we have, and it's one of the only common denominators that we all share as human beings. It is going to happen. I think what scares us is that we don't understand what dying really means. If I were to ask you, what scares you about eternity, you would probably respond, "Well, duh, I'm dead!" Quite the contrary. Your life is just beginning! Once our time is done here on Earth, we will spend eternity somewhere. As I mentioned, there are only two choices: heaven or hell. There is no third or fourth choice, but it still remains your choice. And the only way to get to God in heaven is through His Son, Jesus. There's no other way. There is no back door to sneak you through.

God also knows the exact day and time you will die, so stop worrying about it. God has your days preordained, and you can't do anything to "reordain" them. When you pass away, or, as I prefer to say, pass on, your flesh dies, but your soul immediately passes on to your forever home. Where you are now is just your temporary home. Compared to eternity, your time here is but a vapor, about as much time as it takes you to blink. This is a very quick testing place to determine your forever resting place. That's why we should focus more on our decision about where our eternal home will be. Did I mention that eternity is forever and ever and ever and ever? Okay, I just wanted to drive that point home. I just want you to understand how abbreviated your years are here compared to eternity. I know we all want to succeed in our own ways here on Earth. There's nothing wrong with that. We all need to work and provide for our families. There is also nothing wrong with making a lot of money as long as you have your priorities right. But in a blink, it's all over. What good was all of that if you didn't give any thought to where you are going next? Which again, by the way, is forever. The fact is, most people don't think about this enough or even at all. They just think that when they die, they will automatically go to heaven. That is why the path to heaven is narrow and there is a wide, crowded highway to hell. You must choose one path or the other.

I'm going to hit you with two more words, but don't get nervous. They are easy to understand. Salvation and sanctification. Salvation means being "saved." This happens in a moment's time when you make the decision to accept Jesus as your Savior. Jesus is called your Savior because He died on the cross to "save" you. You cannot earn your salvation. It is a free gift from God upon your decision. Because of your decision, you will now be spending eternity with God in heaven. Sanctification, on the other hand, means living your life in obedience to God out of gratitude for your salvation. It means living your life to become more Christ-like. God begins to work on your heart, and you find yourself wanting to do the right thing more and more. Sanctification (being obedient to God) doesn't get you into heaven. Your decision to be saved gets you into heaven. However, being obedient to God from this point forward may result in greater rewards in heaven.

Begin to live your life for God (i.e., sanctification). Ask God to use His Holy Spirit to guide you into His purposes for your life. This is actually very exciting. You may figure out that your plan is not the same as God's plan. God's plan supersedes your plan every day of the week. It takes some people longer than others to figure out that plan. That's okay. Be patient and keep praying. Besides that, ask God to use you in any way He can to be a blessing to others. God said that His two greatest commandments are to love God and love people (see Matthew 22:36–40). Once you turn your life over to God, these things will start to come naturally. Don't get me wrong—it takes work and discipline. But after a while, it won't feel forced. Just be nice. Put other people before yourself. Treat others as you would want to be treated. Be selfless, not selfish. No matter what it might cost you, always do the right thing. If you do the wrong thing, it will cost you way more than you think down the road. And *always* put God first! Be humble. If God is not too good for you, don't act like you're too good for anybody else. Our lives don't come with owner's manuals, teaching us how to handle every situation. Fortunately, we have the Bible. That is our owner's manual. Any time I have a difficult situation in my life, I just ask myself, "What would Jesus do?" I usually have the answer within seconds.

Let's weigh your options. You can spend eternity with the devil in the fiery pits of hell—forever and ever—that's what eternity means. Or you can spend eternity with God in heaven, in a place that's so spectacular that you would never even be able to dream or imagine anything that would remotely compare to it here on Earth. Hmm . . . I know, tough choice. Well, I don't like the first choice, but what's so good about heaven? First and foremost, God is there. He has also prepared a place for you. He has built you a mansion. You will be completely restored physically, mentally, emotionally, and in every other way. Here is just a short list of things that *won't* be in heaven: grief, sickness, resentment, anxiety, pain, gossip, hatred, jealousy, guilt, sin, tears, strife, bitterness, greed, anger, worry, and stress.

. . .

These are just to name a few. Just about all of us have most, if not all, of these in our lives. What do you think it would be like if *none* of these existed in your life ever again? Wouldn't that be incredible? Not to mention, you could eat whatever you want for eternity and never get fat! Count me in! You will also be reunited with loved ones who made the same choice as you. You may also get to see those beloved pets that you have lost but not forgotten over the years. There will be nothing but smiles and love and happiness. There will be music more beautiful than you have ever heard before. It will be the cleanest, most pristine place you have ever seen. Everybody knows and loves each other, and you never have to "watch your back" for something bad to happen. It will just be total bliss! Of course, the icing on the cake is being in the presence of the Creator of the universe. This is what blows my mind the most. We will get to be face to face, hand in hand, with our Maker. His big strong arms open wide to welcome us and to hug us whenever we want.

You will be in total paradise. So you see that death is nothing to fear. This is actually when you begin to live. Your time on Earth is nothing but a dress rehearsal. Please keep in mind that I cannot even come close to doing heaven justice with my description. As magnificent as I am describing it, multiply that by thousands and we still won't even be in the ballpark of its grandeur. Why would you not want that for yourself, and why would you not want to share that with others?

You know how some people here on Earth reach certain levels in life and they think they've "arrived"? While it's good to feel a certain level of accomplishment, it's even better to realize that this pales in comparison to what "arrived" really means, if you make the right choice. I hope this helps you with your decision, and I pray it moves you enough to want to share Jesus with others so they get a chance to live in paradise with you. Don't wait until it's too late. Your eternity could start tomorrow.

CHAPTER 3
WHAT ABOUT MY PAST?

WHAT ABOUT THE things I've done in my past? There are many people who may be saying, "Yeah, that heaven thing sounds great, but you don't know about my past. You have no idea about some of the things I've done. God can't possibly still love me and want me in heaven." I completely understand that line of thought. I felt the same way. Thankfully, that couldn't be further from the truth. Sin is sin! It doesn't matter how bad it was, or how many times it was, or for how long it went on. I already told you that there will only be one person in the history of the world who would walk this earth and be sin-free, and that was Jesus. We are all sinners, and we will always be sinners until God calls us home. God made us that way. This may surprise you, but God knows about every sin you commit way before it even happens. God hates the sin, but never stops loving the sinner. I really needed to hear that early on. The fact is that none of us are worthy of God's continual forgiveness and unconditional love. That's why He sent His Son, Jesus, to pay the ultimate price for our sins. Isn't that amazing? He sent his only son, Jesus Christ, to shed His blood and to die on the cross, so that our sins could be forgiven, so we could spend eternity with Him in heaven. And He would have done that for you if you were the only person to ever live. Incredible!

As soon as you decide to turn your life over to God, you are now a new person. All of your sins are forgiven, and God wipes them away as if they never even happened. He wipes the slate clean no matter how bad it was. Once He has forgiven that sin, it is forgiven forever. Let it go and stop reminding God about it, and more importantly, stop reminding yourself about it. Stop beating yourself up and move on. Who are we to say that Jesus's death was not enough to erase our sins when God says it is? I needed to work on this. I was my own toughest critic. I'm sure some of you can relate. God's grace is available to everybody. This is not an exclusive club. God won't turn His back on anyone. Let me encourage you. God used some of the most unlikely and disliked people to proclaim His message. He used tax collectors and prostitutes and liars and thieves and adulterers and murderers. Why? So we would be able to relate to those people and know that it's not too late for us, no matter what we've done. Learning that excited me because I was most of the things on that list. Just kidding. But even if I were, God would have forgiven me and given me a fresh start. One of the most popular books in prisons is the Bible. Many men and women turn to God for help and guidance so they can turn their lives around once they get out of prison. Some of them may never get out, yet He uses them anyway to help fellow prisoners. You may be doing life in prison, but you can still do eternity with God. It's not too late for anybody to be saved and to be used by God. It would be very discouraging to all of us if God only used preachers and other popular upstanding citizens as examples. God wants to use each and every one of us for a specific purpose. Use your past as practice and experience for everything that you do from this day forward.

God loves you unconditionally, and He made you exactly the way He wanted you. God doesn't make mistakes. These are some things that God did *not* say about you after He created you:

"Boy did I screw up!"

"What was I thinking?"

"You're beyond repair!"

"You're useless!"

"I can't use you."

"You blew it!"

"You'll never amount to anything!"

"You're too fat, too skinny, too short, too tall, too quiet, too loud, too ugly, the wrong color, the wrong gender!"

. . .

God *never* says any of these things. Some of these were meant to be funny, but I want to be sensitive because some may hit home for you. God would never say or think any of these things, but maybe somebody else in your life has—perhaps somebody very close to you. I know that hurts, but that is certainly not God's opinion of you. God did not "fall asleep at the wheel" while He was creating you. He personally handcrafted you in His image, just the way He wants you. God does not play favorites. Some of us will face more challenges in life than others, but God loves us all the same. God is using those challenges to draw us closer to Him.

The situation you are in right now may not be your fault, but it becomes your fault if you keep feeling sorry for yourself and decide to remain there. I'm not being unsympathetic; I just know that's not what God wants for you. Maybe you didn't have the best parents or the best upbringing. My heart hurts for you because I hate to see or hear that, but do not let your past hold you captive. You are now a new person, once you've accepted Jesus as your Savior. There may have been times when you have felt alone. You will never be alone again. You now have the Holy Spirit of God living inside you. He will never ever leave you. Think about that. From now on, it is not you against the world, as it has felt like for a long time. It is now you and God against the world. I have great news for you: God doesn't lose! With God on your side, He can use you in ways you never thought would be possible.

AN INVITATION FROM GOD

One last thing that God thankfully never says to us: "This is your last chance." If this was God's attitude, none of us would get to heaven. I've told you a couple of times that we are all sinners and we will all be sinners until our days here are up. We are all going to fall short of perfection every single day. God doesn't want or expect perfection. God wants progress. He wants an honest heart. He just wants a relationship with us (and our flaws). We all make mistakes. Mistake is another word for experience or growth. God does not want us to be perfect. He just wants us to acknowledge our mistakes, to take responsibility for them, and to learn and grow from them.

It may be a big stretch for you to think that you can go from an extremely checkered past (if the shoe fits) to being used by God in a big way. You absolutely can, but think more in terms of baby steps. Just talk to God honestly from your heart and ask Him for forgiveness and thank Him for it. Then, ask Him to use you in any way He wants. He'll help you be a better person today than you were yesterday, and a better person tomorrow than you are today. You are better than you think you are. Don't be so hard on yourself. Be patient, and you will be amazed what God will do in your life. It's never too late! Leave your past where it belongs—in the past.

Make the next chapter of your life so great that you have no recollection of pain or regrets from the previous chapters! It's just a decision!

CHAPTER 4
WHAT WILL PEOPLE THINK?

THIS IS a question that cripples most adults, not just when it comes to God but in every area of our lives. We will spend a high percentage of our adult lives living for the acceptance or approval of other people, never giving ourselves a chance to truly enjoy life or to live the way we'd really like to live. We live in a world of rapidly growing technology and social media outlets. Everybody likes to post pictures and videos of themselves and their families in the most perfect situations. You may post a picture of a new car, or a new home, or maybe some type of accomplishment that you or one of your family members has achieved. Or maybe you're posting beautiful family pictures together. Please don't get me wrong. There is absolutely nothing wrong with this. I do it myself. It is much better than publicly "airing your dirty laundry" (which many people do as well). However, a lot of times, we are posting these pictures for approval and acceptance, and sometimes even to impress people. We want to paint a rosy picture because we want people to think a certain way about us, only showing what we want them to see. Meanwhile, behind the scenes, you just beat the cat because you had a bad day. I don't want you to misunderstand me. I love seeing posts like that of people's families and the great things that are happening in their lives. That's much better than all the negative garbage that people are posting. All I'm saying is, at times we may do things for the wrong reasons, and I'm not just talking about what we put on social media. We become prisoners of the opinions of other people. There are actually people who will choose their significant other based on others' approval. It may be about looks. They may know there is no real future with the person, but they want people to see them with someone attractive. They may pick someone (or not pick someone) based on their race, heritage, height, weight, title, financial status, or a number of other superficial qualities, simply because they yearn for the approval of others. This is not a healthy attitude, and it will come with consequences.

Let me ask a quick question here. Think about the people in your life whose opinions mean the most to you or even the people in your life whose opinions you fear the most. It could be a family member, or a close friend, or a neighbor, or a coworker, etc. Are these people in positions where you'd like to be in life? I don't just mean financially, but in every area of their lives. Are they as happy as you would like to be? Do they treat people the way you would treat people? How are their relationships? Do they treat their spouse and their kids the way you would treat yours? Do they have a true foundation, which means a strong relationship with God? If not, why do you care for one second what they think? If you said yes to the questions above, then you would never have to worry about their opinions. In fact, you would welcome them because they would probably encourage you and not judge you. Small-minded people judge you, but truly great people help you become great.

I will be completely honest with you. I lived my life for the approval of others for a long time. I would think, "What will this person think?" and "What will that person say?" and "What if this person knows and that person knows and they get together and talk about me?" I know! Ridiculous, right? If you are thinking that way, and many of us do, let me clear your mind. No offense meant by this, but you are flattering yourself and giving yourself way too much credit to think that these people are giving your life that much thought, or any thought at all. Their lives may be so screwed up that they can barely handle what's going on in their own families—never mind giving yours that much thought. We create so many situations and scenarios in our minds that will never exist in reality. If your biggest concern in life is what people are saying or thinking about you, you will never live the life God created you to live. People will always have their opinions. Don't worry about that. You know what they say about opinions—everybody's got one. People will always have their thoughts about how others should be living their lives. Isn't that amazing?! Most people don't have a clue how to run their own lives, but they are experts on how to run others' lives. Unfortunately, we allow these thoughts to hinder us for the majority of our adult lives. We live our lives based on what we think other people think, when they're probably not thinking about us at all. It sounds so silly, but for some of us, our entire lives will be altered by this silliness.

This is no different when we want to turn our lives over to God and to start living a better life. We again consume ourselves with the potential thoughts of others. I say "potential" because there's a really good chance that no one is having any thoughts of us whatsoever. But even if they are, what's that got to do with your relationship with God? I used to have these worries. Thankfully, God helped me deal with those concerns before I wasted my whole life on them. Once you've accepted Jesus as your Lord and Savior, those worries and fears go away. God helps you deal with them. Eventually I no longer cared about what anybody else thought of me; I only cared about what God thought about me. There is only one opinion that will ever matter, and that is God's. Turning your life over to God is not a stressful event; it's a liberating event. Here's how I live my life now: I care only about what

God *knows* about me and not what people *think* about me. Learning this felt like a giant weight was lifted off my shoulders. I accepted Jesus as my Savior and started living my life for God, not in fear of what other people would think.

What have you got to lose? Friends? Are they really friends then? I became way more excited about the friends I could gain rather than the ones I could lose—and I was even more excited about being God's friend. If somebody wants to stop being your friend because you want a relationship with God, then let them go. Treat them with respect but let them go. Don't let them get between you and your relationship with God. Pray for them but stand your ground. When they really need you, they may come back to you —and to God— because you came back to Him. But if you cower because of their opinion, not only will you blow it for yourself, but you will blow it for them. If you cave because of one person's opinion, you will leave them wondering how important God really is.

You have no idea how many lives you can touch in a positive way if you just stop caring about the opinions of negative people. Consider this: If people don't share your belief, what do you care? What's the worst that could happen to you? You lose someone you thought was a friend? Perhaps. But really that's their loss. Not only are they losing you, but now that you know what you know, think about what they're losing. Think about where they're choosing to spend eternity. All I'm saying is, they are losing a lot more than you are.

Don't spend another second worrying about what other people think or what friends you may lose. Just focus on your relationship with God and get excited about the people who want the same. Just stay strong and be an example. You never know who's watching. You may be surprised to learn that, because you stayed strong with your faith, others are thinking, "If he can believe, then so can I. If he can be saved, so can I." How awesome is that going to be?! Let's switch our thinking to worrying not about the few we may lose but about the many we could help be saved. It is time to remove the shackles of others' opinions so we can live the life God wants us to live and so we can free others as well.

CHAPTER 5
RUN YOUR RACE

THIS MAY BE a close relative of the previous chapter but allow me to expand. Not only do we tend to concern ourselves with what other people may think or say about us, but we also fall into the trap of comparing ourselves to others. We are competing with other people and trying to "keep up" with others around us. Another very dangerous game. What are you chasing anyway? I believe that most of us are chasing what we think society's idea of success is. You've heard of the expression "keeping up with the Joneses." That's the trap we fall into. We buy things we don't need, with money we don't have, to impress people we don't even like. Makes perfect sense to me (*sarcasm*). This is just another desperate attempt for approval and acceptance. Living a fake life instead of the one God wants you to live.

. . .

What is success anyway? This is a really loaded question and completely speculative. You can ask a hundred people this question and get a hundred different answers. The most common thing that pops into people's minds when asked about success is having lots of money. We associate designer clothes, an expensive car, a big beautiful home, expensive jewelry, and a yearly European vacation with success. There's nothing wrong with those things—unless you think that's all success is. If I had to describe success in one word, I think it would be "balance." While many people equate lots of money with success, achieving it may have cost them dearly in other areas of their lives. I don't mean to generalize, but in many cases, people who have a lot of money may not have a lot of free time or time to enjoy life. They are so busy making a living that they don't have a life.

This creates other problems as well. We are jeopardizing our health and happiness when we are stressed out about our workload. Our relationships may suffer because our work continually takes priority. What good is all the money in the world if we don't have our health or we have very little time for our loved ones? Sadly, this type of lifestyle often leads to divorce and barely knowing our children. That is not balance and that is not true success, but we do it to keep up with our neighbors and coworkers and friends, because society has manipulated us into believing this is what we needed to do. We get hung up on the word *status*. We become more intrigued by titles and positions than we do our health and relationships. This is not what God wants. Live your life excited about the titles that God will give you and not some corporation that may not really care about you. Don't misunderstand me. There is nothing wrong with having money. It only becomes wrong when you make money your master—when it becomes all you care about. Money is not good or evil. It is how you earn your money and what you do with it that matters to God.

Once you have accepted Jesus as your Savior, your life can have proper balance. If you haven't, you will always have an unbalanced life, because you will always be giving priority to the wrong things. The key to a balanced life is keeping God first and keeping God in the center of your life. Just by doing this, God will help you balance your life. There is time for work, time for play, time for family, and time for anything else you want *if* you keep God in the center of your life. This will also help you live a happier, healthier, less stressed-out life. Stop comparing yourself to others and what they might have. They might not even be saved. Run your own race! True success is knowing where you will spend eternity and then living the life God wants *you* to live. He does not want you to live the life that you think others think you should live.

Be you. You are an original. There will never be another like you. God made you just the way He wanted you. He designed you for a specific purpose, a purpose that no one else ever created can fulfill. God so masterfully created you that He also designated a purpose that could only be carried out by you. I hope you are ecstatic about that. No more competing. No more comparing. No more trying to keep up. I saw a really cool quote once that said, "The only competition you have is with the person you were yesterday." Don't try to compete with anybody else.

Now just get locked in with God to figure out what His purpose is for your life. He will help you with this. None of us were haphazardly created just to exist and do nothing. There is a reason for every one of us being here, and part of the fun is figuring out what that reason is. You are not a mistake. You may have been a mistake, or, let me put it a nicer way, a surprise to your parents, but you are no surprise to God. You were conceived in God's mind long before your parents conceived you. You were conceived in God's mind long before your parents even met. God had you conceived in His mind since before He created the universe. Here's how special and unique you are. God created this massive universe and all the beautiful things in it. He also created billions of people who will occupy this earth. With all of that, He still thought that this world would not be complete without you in it. That is astounding. There are no mistakes walking this earth. Don't ever think that you are a mistake!

The only thing left to figure out is what God's purpose for your life is. You are going to need to talk to

God about this. I don't want you to say, "My purpose is to make a lot of money." That is not your purpose. First of all, that's a goal, not a purpose. Second of all, if that was a purpose, that would be your purpose, not God's. God never created anyone for the sole purpose of making a lot of money. God gave every one of us specific gifts, talents, or abilities. You need to figure out what those are and match them up with God's purposes for you. Some of us are musically inclined or have a great voice, while others may be gifted athletically. Some may be very artistic, while others are great on the computer. Use what God has given you to fulfill His purposes. God won't give you a purpose without giving you the corresponding ability to fulfill that purpose. If you can't carry a tune to save your life, you're probably not supposed to be a singer. If you're not sure which end of a screwdriver to use, you're probably not supposed to be working with your hands in construction. If you're really clumsy and are constantly tripping over your own feet, ballroom dancing may not be in your future. If you're not technologically savvy, then computer work may not be for you. I'm all of about five feet, two inches tall. I realized early in my life that I was not called to play in the NBA.

You get my point. Every single one of us does have some talent or ability that we can use, though. It doesn't have to be something work related either. Maybe you'd like to donate your time working with children or with the elderly at retirement homes. You might love animals and want to work with them in some capacity. Whatever the case may be, try to figure out what you love to do and what God gave you the ability to do. You don't need any more than what God's given you, but you need to use *all* of what He's given you. Most importantly, God wants you to be you. He doesn't want you to be like anybody else, or He would have made you that way. Learn to embrace how God made you and to love who you are, understanding that God couldn't be more thrilled with His creation of you. Live your life with the peace of knowing that God is saying to you, "Just use the gifts that I've given you to run your race, and I've got the rest."

CHAPTER 6
WHAT IS FAITH?

FAITH ACTUALLY HAS a couple of different meanings, but to some degree, we all have it. If you don't agree, I would ask you a few questions. Have you ever been on an elevator? Or on an airplane? Or on a ride at an amusement park? Or on a cruise? Or in a car? Of course I could go on and on about things we do every day that take a certain degree of faith. Working at an auto repair garage for many years, I had faith that the lift holding up the cars I was working underneath wouldn't collapse. Think about the amount of faith that you have just driving your car every day. You have faith that your vehicle is mechanically sound and won't break down or fall apart on you. You have faith that you will stay focused enough to keep yourself safe while you're driving. You also have faith that the thousands of other drivers on the road are sober and are completely focused on the road and paying attention to nothing else. Ha ha ha ha! What a joke that is.

This world we live in today, with technology and cell phones, makes it extremely dangerous to be on the road at all. So many people are so distracted by their cell phones and their music, they forget they're even driving. It amazes me what "activities" people are engaged in when they're supposed to be driving their car. This one's on the phone, that one's doing their makeup, the other one's eating a burger, and there's the car full of kids who look like they're having a dance party. I'm no saint—I've done a couple of these. That's why thousands of people get killed every day by distracted drivers. But we don't even give it one second thought before we jump in our cars and go somewhere. That's called faith. I highly doubt that you would be all excited about taking a car ride if you thought for one second that you might be killed by a drunk driver or a distracted driver. Yet it happens thousands of times a day. You know this, but you have total faith that it's not going to happen to you. This is just when driving your car. I will not beat this to death by elaborating on all of the other examples. I'm sure you get the point. There are many things we do every single day, things that we never even think about, that take some level of faith.

Faith also has a similar meaning to a word that seems like its opposite, and that's fear. Fear and faith both mean believing in something unseen, or believing in something that hasn't happened yet. Although they have similar meanings, the one you choose to live your life by makes all the difference in the world. Fear is a negative expectation—an expectation that something bad is going to happen. Faith here, has a similar meaning to hope, which is a positive, joyful expectation or anticipation that something good is going to happen. Fear and faith can sometimes clash in your body at the same time. It is crucial to let faith run your life and not fear. I'm not saying this is easy. Life is going to throw all kinds of things at you, but what good does it do to live in fear? What good does it do to worry all the time? It does absolutely no good. In fact, the more you worry about things, the more likely they are to happen. Just like when you expect good things to happen, the more likely good things are bound to happen.

Faith is not always logical. It consists of believing in things that haven't transpired yet, as if they already have. This will become clearer as you grow in your relationship with God. And once you have God in your life, what is there to fear? You have God on your side. All of your battles now become God's. He just wants you to trust Him. God says to cast all of your cares on Him and He will take care of them. That means: stop worrying. Leave all of the worrying up to God, and He will deal with it. How cool is that? But you need to trust Him and let it go. If you continue to be consumed by fear and worry, you have allowed those things to conquer your faith, rather than conquering fear and worry by your faith.

Another example of faith pertains to your spiritual life. Faith also means to have a strong confidence and trust in your belief in God. Pretty basic, right? Then why did this word scare me too? If you would have said to me years ago about someone else, "He is a person of faith," I would have thought for sure that meant he walked around in a robe all day trying to bless people. Another silly misconception. I have never worn a robe in my life, and I still have a very strong faith. I have total confidence and an unwavering belief in God, which has led me to a personal relationship with Him. That's it. Nothing too heavy. Be excited about having faith. Faith is a gift from God. It takes faith to go to heaven. You are saved by God's grace through your faith. You've heard the expression "having childlike faith." This means a child is very trusting, teachable, and humble. They also have a strong reliance on an adult figure or figures in their life. God wants the same from you. He wants you to have childlike faith when it comes to your relationship with Him. He wants you to be humble and teachable. He also wants you to rely fully on Him. This does not mean that you sit in your lazy chair every day and say, "God, go to work. I'm relying on you." God is going to do things not *for* you but *with* you. God is not going to steer your parked car. He wants you to be fully involved in the process. The Bible says faith without works is dead. It also says in the Bible that if you have the faith of a mustard seed, you can move mountains and nothing will be impossible for you. God uses the example of a mustard seed because it is one of the tiniest grains in the world. If you can move mountains with the faith of a mustard seed, think about what could happen if you had a lot of faith. Remember, when you have this kind of faith, you now have the Holy Spirit living inside you. You literally have God living inside you. Don't doubt yourself or your abilities ever again. From now on, remember, using the words "I can't" is the same as saying "God can't." God is now with you everywhere you go, and "with God all things are possible" (Matthew 19:26 NIV).

CHAPTER 7
WILL I STILL HAVE STRUGGLES?

I WOULD LIKE to tell you that now that you have God in your life, your struggles are over. But I'd be lying. God never promised us a struggle-free life. He did promise us that He would be there with us through those struggles. That is the best part about accepting Jesus as your Lord and Savior. He is now living inside you, and He will never ever leave you. What you used to have to deal with on your own, you can now handle with the Creator of the universe. To say this puts you on a level playing field would be an insult to God. You were pretty much on a level playing field before making the greatest decision of your life. Now that you've made that decision, the scale is tilted heavily in your favor. God is now working on your behalf to fight your battles. In fact, they're no longer your battles, they're God's. And God doesn't lose. Yes, you will still have difficult and challenging situations, but God has a purpose for them. He's trying to teach you something or shape you for a job He has for you. He allows these situations and will walk through them with you. This should bring you great peace. Situations that seemed monumental in the past, you will realize are a cakewalk for God. That does not mean life becomes a cakewalk. It means we are all going to go through many struggles in our lives, with or without God. Trust me, they are a lot easier with God, knowing that He has allowed them for a reason and that He's in control. I really don't even like to imagine what I would do without God in my life. What would I do when life gets really hard: Cross my fingers? Make a wish? Leave it to chance? No thanks.

Accepting God in your life also doesn't mean that things are going to go exactly how you want or expect them to go. This is actually a good thing. You will begin to understand that God will close doors in your life that He wants closed, and He will open doors that He wants opened. Most times, we don't understand God's plan until later, if at all. We may feel like we are going through an absolute nightmare, only to realize later that we had to go through that nightmare to get to God's dream for our lives. There is a saying around Christmas that says, "Remember the reason for the season." The Bible talks about challenging times in your life as "seasons." I would encourage you to remember that there are reasons for all of those seasons as well. God doesn't make bad things happen in your life, but He will allow certain things to happen. Rest assured, when God allows these things to happen, it is always for your benefit. Although these things hurt at the time, He will never waste your pain. This allowed me to change my entire outlook on life. Now when bad things happen, I ask myself, *Why did God allow this to happen?* instead of *Why did God do this to me?* My attitude went from blaming God to giving God credit and seeking His purposes. God always knows best.

I need to give you a quick personal story. I had just turned fifty years old and was married for twenty-four years. My wife and I had known each other since high school, so by the time I was fifty, we had known each other for thirty-five years. That is 70 percent of my life. It was at this time that she informed me she no longer wanted to be married. This came out of nowhere, and I was completely shocked and devastated. I went into a depression and lost ninety pounds in eight months. This was the darkest time of my life. I do not tell you this for sympathy or for you to think badly about her. We have a twenty-four-year-old son and a twenty-one-year-old daughter together. Thankfully, we remained friendly, despite some choice words and once the initial shock subsided. I tell you this because my life has gone in a completely different direction than I ever thought it would have. Not just with my marriage, but my whole life-purpose.

I told you I have been a blue-collar worker my whole life. My wife works in corporate America. At this stage of our lives, I figured on starting to plan for retirement. Sell the house and downsize. Start to sock money away. Travel to places we always wanted to go, and just "ride it out" at work for as long as I needed to in order to retire. I hate to put it this way, but part of most people's retirement plans is hoping they don't outlive their money. Needless to say, God had different plans. It was during this really dark time that God filled me in on His purpose for my life. I was deeply depressed one day and completely hungover when God woke me from my misery and told me to write a book. I was partly in shock and partly excited—but mostly excited. I ran upstairs (really I was crawling in pain) and started writing. Writing has been my passion since, and I will do it until God tells me to do something else or until He calls me home. God also told me that I will be doing inspirational speaking, and I am so excited about that. Keep in mind, up to this point, I had never had any thoughts or desires about writing. As I've mentioned, my whole working career had been spent at auto repair garages, construction sites, and bars. After thirty-five years in those places, I could have written a book, but it certainly wouldn't have been about God.

Please understand that God is in control. I'll be honest: during that time in my life, I couldn't help but wonder why God would do this *to* me. I never realized that later I would be thanking Him for doing this *for* me. I cringe to think about where my life would have gone if God hadn't allowed certain things, seemingly horrific things, to happen in my life. I most likely would have just "ridden it out" with work, tried my best to retire, and lived like everybody else lives. I don't mean that to be offensive. What I mean is, I would have just lived an average life, never becoming what God intended me to be, never fulfilling His purposes for my life. I would have just existed. But God always knows best. God's plans for your life are always better than your plans. Once you know and love God, He will work to turn your struggles into good. I grew so much closer to God during this time. How can you put a price on that? This is what God wants. This is why He allows struggles. He wants you to rely on Him. He wants you to get closer to Him and for you to trust that He is there.

Before we know God, many of our struggles are self-inflicted. We think we know everything and that we can do everything on our own. How's that working for you? Is your way working? Are you done banging your head against the wall trying to figure out why it's not working your way? I hope so. God is the one and only answer. He is the only One who can help you through all of it. God will never give you too much to handle if you keep Him first and let Him help you. You'll find that He can handle the things that you can't. Difficult times are definitely not fun at the time. We will all go through them. Some things are worse than others. But these struggles are what make us who we are. They will shape us into who God wants us to become. What doesn't kill you makes you stronger. Your most valuable lessons in life come from adversity. No struggle, no victory!

Those struggles can be used to help others when they deal with similar situations. Never in a million years would I have thought that I'd be able to speak firsthand about what it feels like to go through a divorce. I was so proud of my marriage and was crazy about her right until the end. Now I may be able to help others who are going through the same thing. Do you see why it's futile to try to figure this out on your own? God will use you in ways you would never dream of on your own. I love that! I'm not saying that you should go to bed tonight and pray for problems. No need for that. They will find you on their own. I just want you to look at them differently now. Challenges equal experience and wisdom. Challenges equal opportunity. Don't question God. Question yourself. Ask yourself why God may be allowing your challenges. Talk to God. Ask Him to help you understand the reason for the season. In a period of one year, my life did a complete turnaround from where I thought it was going, and I couldn't be more excited about it now. God is so good!

CHAPTER 8
MAKE GOD YOUR BFF

IF I WERE to ask you what qualities a best friend possesses, what would you say? You might use words like loyal, loving, trustworthy, reliable, selfless, fun, and compassionate. Or you may use phrases like "They would do anything for me," "They're always there for me," "They're a really good listener," "I can tell them anything," "They always have my back," or "They really 'get' me." You may even go through crazy things in life and that one person is always with you through it all. They are the only one who understands you and the things that have gone on in your life. They know your deepest secrets. People like this are very important to have in your life. They really make life easier and more enjoyable. Many people have someone who they would consider a best friend, or BFF (Best Friend Forever). This is your go-to person when things are good or bad. This is the person, whenever something happens in your life, whom you need to talk to about it. You may even share a secret handshake (is that still a thing?).

There is absolutely nothing wrong with having friends like this. Friendships are key to enjoying life. God created us to have relationships. We were meant to coexist. We were not meant to live or die alone. I have been out of high school for thirty-five years and still have many close friends from back then. My parents and four brothers are still with us. I have a great relationship with all of them, which I am very grateful for. I wouldn't trade any of them for the world. The only problem is that they are in the world, and people who are in the world will let you down from time to time. This is not usually intentional, but it is unavoidable. We are human. None of us can be a perfect friend, or a perfect anything, all the time. As much as we'd like to, we cannot even be there for even our best friend all the time. I don't think there can be a stronger love than the love you have for your children, and you can't even be there for them all the time either. But guess who can? Come on, you know. Of course, God can.

As great as your friends and family are, God is the only one who is not capable of hurting you, intentionally or unintentionally. As I said, He may allow some unpleasant things to happen in your life, but that is always for your own good, because He loves you deeper than anyone else ever could. He is the only one who is there for you every second of every day (even when you're sleeping). He is the only one who truly

AN INVITATION FROM GOD

knows what's best for you and can actually make it happen. He is the only one who will forgive you immediately no matter how many times you fall short, and He never holds a grudge. He is the only one who can handle your troubles and, quite frankly, the only one who wants to. He is the only one who knows your every thought and your deepest secrets. He is the only one who really "gets" you. He is the only one who can align things and people in your life for your benefit. He is the only one who can protect you and your family from things that you can't. He protects you from things you may never know about until you meet Him. I pray for protection over my family every day because I can't always be there with them. And even if I could be there with them twenty-four hours a day, I still can't do what God can do. I can't stop a drunk driver from hitting them. I can't hold a deer back from running in front of their car late at night. I can't keep them from getting sick, or healing them if they do. But God can. There are countless ways that God and His angels are protecting you and your loved ones every day, and you may never give it a second thought. I thank God every day for that protection, and I never want to take it for granted.

God is so good and can do things that no one else could do, even if they wanted to. God has more thoughts about you every day than there are grains of sand on the beach. Think about how powerful that is. You are always on God's mind, and He wants to be your friend. God is yearning to be your friend. Not only does He want to be your friend, but He wants you to be His friend. He doesn't only want to be a friend to you, but He wants you to be a friend to Him. How humbling is that? I hope you can grasp the magnitude of that. Picture a little kid at a playground going up to another kid and saying, "Will you be my friend?" How heartwarming is that? Well, this is what God is saying to you. He just wants to be your friend. The Creator of the universe is asking you to be His friend. This blew my mind. Just so you know, I accepted His friend request, and I hope you will too. This is when I started to view our relationship differently. Not only do I ask God to do things for me, but I also ask what I can do for Him, just like a friend would do. He is still God, and I treat Him that way. I can never do for Him what He can do for me or, more importantly, what He has already done for me. I am not His equal, and I'm very respectful about that. I just want God to know that I am serious about our friendship and that I'd do anything for Him. I don't want to beat this point to death, but I want you to get this. Jesus completely humbled Himself and fulfilled God's will for His life. He was mocked, insulted, humiliated, and tortured. He shed His blood on the cross so that your sins could be forgiven, so that you could spend eternity in heaven with Him. He did that so you could have an eternal friendship with Him. He also gave you the chance to share that opportunity with others. Total and complete humility.

. . .

AN INVITATION FROM GOD

How do you make God your best friend? Pray often. God is always there. No appointment necessary! Be yourself. Talk to Him all the time. That's all praying is. It does not need to be fancy. If it did, I would have been eliminated. I don't know how to be fancy—I only know how to be me, and that's all God wants. There is no such thing as a bad pray-er. The only bad pray-er is one who doesn't pray. Just be completely honest. Confess to God when you screw up. You do not need a liaison between you and God to confess your sins to. Confession is between you and God. You have a direct line to God, and there is no third party required. He already knows your heart and everything there is to know about you. He just wants you to open up to Him, and to trust Him, and to share with Him what He already knows. He just wants your friendship. What would it be like if your children decided to stop talking to you? What if they wanted no relationship with you whatsoever? How would that make you feel? You assisted in giving them life, and now they want nothing to do with you? How can that be? How do you think God feels if we do that to Him? He feels the same way. God longs for that relationship with you. Isn't that so cool? Include God in everything you do. Invite Him into every area of your life. He's already there anyway, so why not invite Him in and make Him feel welcome. Make God your business partner, your relationship counselor, your financial planner, your dietician, etc. Your success rate will be so much higher if you include God in everything you do.

Making God your best friend does not diminish your relationship with others; it actually enhances it. Remember, we were created for relationships with other people. Your relationship with God will make you a better spouse, parent, friend, co-worker, and neighbor. In short, all your relationships will improve. You will become more compassionate, more supportive, more understanding, more accepting, more forgiving, more encouraging, and more loving, just to name a few. You will begin to live every day for God, and fewer things will bother you—and things will bother you less. Even if you hate your job, your attitude will change about work. You now have the mind-set that you're doing your job for God and not for a boss, or a corporation, or even just for a paycheck. When you talk to God and keep your attitude right, God will get you out of that situation if that's His will. Do everything like you're doing it for God, and you will be so blessed.

It is okay to ask God for things. If you don't ask, you won't receive. It is also okay to pray bold prayers and ask for big things. The Bible says to come before God boldly with confidence, which should never be confused with cockiness and arrogance. Make your prayers so big that they can't be accomplished without God's help. Why ask for small things that you could do on your own? But even if I could do small things on my own, I wouldn't want to. Everything is better when

AN INVITATION FROM GOD

God's involved, and nothing is too small or too big for God. God answers all prayers. His answer to your prayers will either be "Yes," "No," or "Not now." But He always knows best. Now you get to be God's friend as well. You know how people like to brag about having friends in high places? Nobody can "one-up" you here. You can't go any higher than God! Open up to God and welcome your new best friend with open arms, like He has always been doing for you. Ask Him to use you in ways only you can be used. Ask Him to help you reach people only you can reach. I can't imagine living my life without God, but I also couldn't imagine not living my life *for* God. Live your life so God will say, "I knew I could count on you!"

CHAPTER 9
WHO AM I NOW?

YOU MIGHT BE THINKING, *Now that I've accepted God into my life, who am I?* Let me answer that question with a question. Who do you want to be? Everybody else is already taken. You have no choice but to be you. Stop trying to be somebody else. God created you to be you and nobody else. Because you now have God in your life, you've just become a better version of you—but still you. You are God's masterpiece, and He is not confused about who He wants you to be. He did not make a mistake. He just wants you to be the best you that you can be. You will be changed as a person for the better, but God does not want you to change who you are at the core. He just wants you to chip away at the bad stuff and allow the good stuff to be more prevalent. Your personality and characteristics are a gift from God, and He does not want you to lose that or to try to be somebody different. You are an individual. There is nobody that is exactly like you, and there never will be. Start to live your life for who He created you to be. You are the same you, but with purpose and passion.

There is nothing drastic that you need to do once you've accepted Jesus. You don't need to wear special clothes. You don't need to wear special jewelry. You don't need to put stickers all over your car. You don't need to make an announcement. You don't need to go around anointing people. Just be you. The best part about having God in your life is that your attitude about things starts to change. Not because you're trying, but because that's what God does. Remember, He is now living inside you, and He is with you everywhere you go, so He will subconsciously be changing you for the better. Although God does not want you to change who you are, He will be changing you Himself, and He will want you to make some adjustments to some habits that you may have. These habits, maybe even addictions, may include excessive drinking or drug use, bad language, pornography, gossiping, complaining, unforgiveness, or any other lifestyles or negative traits that don't line up with what God wants for your life. Relax! We all have them, and change doesn't happen overnight. This is a process—a forever process. Don't dread the process, enjoy it. Be patient with yourself. You don't need to change your whole life overnight. God knows your weaknesses. He just wants you to recognize them and to ask for help fixing them. Don't be ashamed. He already knows. If you want to live in God's favor, you have to be for what God's for and against what He's against. You can't be for what He's against and against what He's for. Well, you can be, but not if you want to be in God's graces. It was okay before you knew any better, but not now that you know. Take God's side like He takes yours.

You will never do everything right, and you will never be perfect. God is not looking for perfect. Perfection is unattainable, so stop shooting for it. Do you know how hard it is to go just one day without sinning? Even on our best days, things happen. You may not even know it happened. Possibly an angry or hateful thought. Or maybe you lost your temper and a four-letter word slipped out. You could have had feelings of jealousy or envy. Did you complain or gossip? You may have had an impure thought and maybe even acted on it. Much of this is not intentional, but it does occur. Every day when I pray, I tell God, *Lord, I know I'm a sinner and I sin every day, but I'm working every day on making myself more like who you want me to be. Please help me.* God doesn't expect you to be anywhere near perfect; He expects an honest effort toward obedience. Do your best every day to live your life by God's two greatest commandments: love God, and love others as yourself. The rest will fall into place.

It is so incredible to see the changes that start to take place. You will actually feel God working in your life. Embrace the changes. As your relationship with God grows stronger, an amazing thing starts to happen. Your

AN INVITATION FROM GOD

whole nature changes and you begin to feel alive. Your attitude will shift from not wanting anybody to know about this to wanting to share it with the world. (Remember, at your own pace and when you're ready.) Your character will develop. Doing the right thing will become instinctive. Your integrity will begin to shine. You will forgive people more quickly. Complaining will begin to fade, and gratitude will take a front seat. You will become thankful for everything in your life and take fewer things for granted. You will develop a new level of appreciation for life and begin to realize how awesome it really is. You will find yourself complimenting and encouraging people. You will now be able to see the good in everything and everybody, instead of the bad. Will you still have bad days? That's up to you. Bad things will still happen, but your attitude will make those things seem not so monumental anymore. What you used to consider a bad day, you now consider another day of growth and another step closer to God.

When you really start to understand what you've got, you develop a new level of boldness. Not arrogance, but boldness. Stay humble. My dad taught me something about humility when I was younger. He said, "If you're that good at something, other people will talk about you. You don't need to do your own bragging." That always stuck with me. This doesn't mean you can't be proud of your accomplishments; just don't break your arm patting yourself on the back in front of people. The only boasting I ever do is about

God and how great He is. I give God credit for everything. Any accomplishments I have ever achieved came from the abilities God gave me in order to achieve them. I have no self-made abilities. He gets all the honor and glory. I never want to steal God's thunder. Don't take credit for what God's done in your life.

You might wonder, *Can I still have fun?* No. Now that the greatest thing in your life has happened, it's time to be miserable. Just kidding (scared you, didn't I?). Of course you can still have fun. God created us to have fun and to laugh, as long as it's not at the expense of others. God wants you to be happy. In no way does accepting God into your life mean that the fun stops. God encourages laughter. Laughter is truly the best medicine (after God Himself). The Bible talks about the beautiful sound of children laughing. Life is not meant to be taken so seriously. It is meant to be joyful. Can you imagine if you were walking around looking all serious or miserable, and somebody asked you, "What's wrong with you?" And you responded, "Oh, don't mind me. I just found God." Are you kidding me? Do you think that's what God wants? What kind of a representation would that be? Instead, you will be noticeably different to people, but in the most incredible way. There will be a new hop in your step. A certain glow in your personality. You will have a much better attitude toward everything. You will wake up in the morning grateful for another day, rather than dreading another day's routine. Nothing will seem to bother you. There will be a sense of peace that you have never experienced before. You'll be more encouraging, joyful, and upbeat. This will come naturally. You won't need to force it or to overdo it in an annoying way. It will come off as genuine. Now people will ask you, "What's gotten into you?" And you can respond, "God!"

CHAPTER 10
GOD'S NOT DONE WITH YOU

IF YOU WOKE up this morning, then God's not done with you. There is still something left for you to do. Have you any idea how many people didn't get that gift of another day today? In 2018, the average death rate worldwide was 157,123 people per day.[1] If you multiply that times 365 days, that's over fifty-seven million people who died that year, and it's close to that every year. And you weren't one of them. Every morning that your eyes open, before your feet even hit the floor, you should thank God for another day. You are not supposed to wake up in the morning cursing another day that you have to endure. That is a slap in the face to God. He gave you the gift of another day, one that many people did not get, and your reaction is, "Oh no, not another day"? If that's your attitude, that needs to change, and it will now that you have God in your life. I totally understand not wanting to go to a job every day that you despise, or having to deal with many other challenges that life throws at you. That's why you need to find your purpose. You need to figure out what God wants to do with you. Once you figure out what God's plan is, you will be springing out of bed in the morning.

Here's how I know that God knows best. I need to get serious for just a moment. When I went through that very difficult time in my life, I was so crushed and depressed that I prayed to God to take me in my sleep. Not just once, but every night for several months. I wasn't going to kill myself, but I didn't think I could handle the pain for much longer. I knew that there is no pain in heaven, and I just wanted it to end. That is a sad way to live, and it is completely opposite of my normal attitude toward life. Up to that point in my life, I was the happiest person ever. Since that time, I have become even happier. Why? Because I found my purpose. I found it during my darkest days, when I needed to lean on God the most. I told you that God always answers prayers: yes, no, or not now. Thank God He said no to that one! Not because I'm not looking forward to meeting Him in person, but because I hadn't fulfilled His purposes for my life yet. Now that's all I live my life for. Before my divorce, I just wanted to settle down and plan for retirement. I had no real future goals, and I actually felt pretty empty, like I hadn't done enough to make a difference or to leave a mark on this world. I did not feel fulfilled. It was at this time, this seemingly tragic time, that God came to me with my life's purposes. This is when my life started to make sense and I knew that everything was going to be alright. I was fifty years old, and my mind-set turned to this: I am fifty years old and still have the other half of my life in front of me. The first fifty years was for experience and wisdom to prepare me for the next fifty years. Now I have fifty years of goals, and retirement isn't one of them. Why? Purpose! It's never too late to figure out God's purposes for your life. It's never too late to start over. I am now fifty-two years old, and I'm just getting started.

If you're still here, then God still has plans for you. Plans that were designated just for you—not somebody like you—you! He has a master plan for your life that only you can carry out. God does not have identical plans for anybody else. God did not take the cookie-cutter approach—one plan fits all. This is amazing, because now you don't need to compete with somebody else's plan. Everybody has their own. You just have to figure out yours. God is absolutely thrilled with your individuality. Use that individuality for God's purposes for your life. Don't worry if you don't know what that is yet. It will take some people longer than others. Don't do what other people say you should do with your life. It's your life, and you only get one shot at it.

This may not be a popular opinion, but since I'm the one writing, I'm gonna give it to you anyway. I don't like to see kids going to college just for the sake of going to college, or because somebody told them they had to, or because they felt like there was no other option at the time. They also might be going because they heard the ridiculous misconception that "you're nothing without a college degree." Tell that one to God. Show me one place in the Bible where it says you need to have a college degree to fulfill God's purposes for your life. Don't get me wrong, I am not against going to college. Both of my kids went to college. I am against being *forced* to go and going for the wrong reasons. How many kids actually know what they want to do for the rest of their lives at seventeen and eighteen years old? Not many. That's why they are coming out of college with a degree that they have no idea how to use. It's one thing if your heart is set on doing something that requires that degree, like a doctor, nurse, lawyer, accountant, or any other specific career. It's another thing to go because somebody told you to go because you're nothing without that degree or because you need it to be "successful." Now you're paying for that degree for half of your working life and may not even be working in the field you got that degree in. But even if you are, are you fulfilling God's purposes for your life? I don't mean this to be insulting, but anybody can work a job. There's a big difference between making a living and living for a purpose. Don't confuse your career with your purpose. You really start to live when you discover your purpose. It's completely awesome if you love your job and your career. If you do, you're ahead of the game. It's also okay if you feel like your career is your calling. There's nothing wrong with any of this. I just want you to live your life and not let anybody live it for you.

Every single one of us has something to contribute to this world. It doesn't have to be anything massive, but it can be. God wants to use all of us for something. None of us is here just by happenstance. If you're still here, you're still useful to God and His people. At first I had no idea how God was going to use me. I was not "most likely to succeed." I dropped out of college. I've been a blue-collar worker my whole adult life. I love sports and would consider myself athletically inclined. However, at my height, professional sports was not an option. That didn't mean that God couldn't use me for something else. I may not be tall, but I have a big heart and a giant God, so nothing is out of reach. The same is true for you. We were all given talents and abilities. God just wants you to use those talents and abilities to make the world a better place and draw people to Him.

Don't give up. The world needs you more than ever right now. As I am writing this, the world is a crazy place. We are in the midst of a global pandemic (COVID-19). If that wasn't enough, there are major conflicts going on right now. What used to be people's opinions and beliefs has now turned into hatred and war: political wars, religious wars, racial wars, economic wars; countries are at war; and people all over the world are at war with each other because of differences of opinions. This is not what God wanted. Every land in the world is God's land. We are all God's people. We are all brothers and sisters in God. I don't want to turn this into gloom and doom; I just want you to know that you can make a difference. Even if it's just to spread peace, pay a compliment, encourage someone, give a smile, be a good example, love people, and, most of all, share God. Think about how much better this world would be if everyone had a personal relationship with God. You can help with that. You can't get to everybody, but you can get to some—and then they can reach others. There are places in the world where you can't talk about God or you'll get thrown in jail or even killed. They would do anything to be able to talk about God, but they can't. We need to be the voice for those people as well. God is the answer for everything. There is nothing that God can't fix.

Okay, let's lighten up a little bit. All I'm saying is, you do count, and God's not done with you. God does want to use you or you wouldn't still be here. That's why God doesn't take you home to heaven as soon as you turn your life over to Him. He was patient with you, and He left you here until you made the decision to be saved. You can thank Him when you see Him because He "saved" you from spending eternity in hell. Now that you have made that decision and are saved, why doesn't He take you now? Because He's not done with you! Now that you're a new creation, He wants to use you for His purposes and to make this world a better place. He wants you to use *all* your talents and abilities, no matter how big or small they are, to fulfill His purposes for your life. We all have talents and abilities. We just need to ask God to help us tap into them and learn how to use them to glorify Him. There are no second chances. There are no do-overs. This is it. Make a difference. Be a shining light. Let the world see that there's something different about you. Have an attitude of gratitude. Don't waste what God has given you. I don't know about you, but when it comes time to meet God, I don't want to make excuses for why I didn't fulfill His purposes for my life, when He fully equipped me with the talents and abilities needed to fulfill them. Don't take one day for granted. Tomorrow is promised to nobody. Live every day like it's your last. Live like you're about to die, but don't die before you start to live. Make every second count.

CHAPTER 11
WHAT NOW?

OKAY, so your next question might be, "Now that I've made the most important decision of my life, what do I do next?" I'm so glad you asked. First of all, congratulations on making that decision. Welcome to your fresh start. I am so happy for you, and you will not regret it. The most important thing now is to do things at your own pace. There's nothing wrong with jumping right in, but there's also nothing wrong with taking it slow. Ask God for help. Spend time every day in prayer. You don't need to set a timer for this. You don't need to pray for a specific amount of time, or at a designated time, or a certain amount of times per day. You can talk to God at any time, for as short or long a time as you want. That's the great part about God: He's always there, and He's always listening. Get comfortable talking to God. Be honest with God. If it's been a while since you've prayed, let Him know. Yes, He already knows (your number hasn't shown up on His caller ID in a while), but God loves honesty and humility. Let Him know about the new life you want to live, and ask Him to guide you through it. There is absolutely nothing to be nervous about. In fact, you have no idea how happy you've made God. His Spirit is hugging you right now, and He is crying tears of joy. His arms and ears are wide open to you.

It is imperative to make this your journey and nobody else's. This is not a competition. Don't try to "outpray" anybody. There is no set amount of prayer time that God requires in order for Him to pay attention to you. I would recommend talking to God every day, though. Always make time for God. Remember that God's your friend and He wants you to know that. This may seem a little awkward at first, but as you get more comfortable, it becomes second nature. You are simply having a conversation with God, your new BFF. You don't need to be kneeling down or in a church to talk to God. God wants to hear from you every day and doesn't expect you to be in church every day. God hears you no matter where you are. You can talk to God when you're driving in your car, or when you're at work, or when you're at the gym, or even when you're at the beach. There's never a wrong time to talk to God. There are times when I'm at work or driving in my car, and I just take a couple of minutes to say hello to God. You know how you have blue-tooth in your car and you're on the phone with your friends constantly? No phone or Bluetooth needed when talking to God. You have a direct line, and there are no dead zones. He hears everything. My prayer when I'm working or driving in my car may be as simple as this: *Hello, my Father in heaven. I just want to thank You for this day. Thank You for all of the blessings in my life, most of all, for Your love and friendship. Please keep my family protected, and please use me in any way to glorify You, Your name, and Your kingdom. Thank You, Lord. I love You. I pray this in Jesus's name. Amen.* This is not word for word, and it's never the same. And you don't need to make my prayer your prayer. There is no perfect template or formula for prayer. I just want you to understand how easy it is. It does not need to be elaborate; it just needs to be you. God wants to hear from you all the time, not just when something goes wrong and when you need something. That's okay, too, but God wants you to be in touch all the time, just like you would want from your children. Like a child would do, there are times when I ask God if I can climb up on His lap so He can hold me while I'm praying. He never says no, and it's amazing how safe and close to Him I feel.

It would be a good idea to become part of a local church, but I would choose carefully. There are many different types of Christian churches. Some Christian churches, like the one I go to, are nondenominational

Christian Bible churches. Just like there are some mechanics, lawyers, and plumbers, etc. who don't do the right thing, unfortunately the same goes for churches. No church is perfect, because there are people there. But I would strongly recommend that whatever one you choose, make sure it is a Bible-believing, Bible-teaching church. One that actually teaches and explains Scripture. With the internet these days, you can easily research churches in your area without having to visit each one. Most church websites have a tab that says, "What We Believe." Make sure they believe that the Bible is true and that they teach from it every week. Watch an online sermon to see what the pastor is preaching. Find a place where you are comfortable, a place that makes you feel at home. You may have to attend a few churches before you find the one that fits you, and that's fine.

Once you're comfortable somewhere, find a mentor, somebody you feel safe talking to about your new journey. It could even be the pastor, but it doesn't have to be. You may find someone in your new church you really hit it off with. Someone you can relate to and have a lot in common with. This doesn't need to happen the first week. Make friends. Build relationships. You'll know when you've found the person you can confide in, the one who can guide you along this path. My older brother is a pastor in Texas, and He is my "go-to" person whenever I have questions or just want to talk about God. As happy as God is with His new friendship with you, He doesn't want you to go it alone. It is key to have relationships with fellow believers. They are there to support you, and guide you, and to build you up. This is what true friends do. What's really amazing is that you will become that friend and that support for somebody else down the road, when they are looking for a new life and a new home. You don't have to be the pastor to be a friend or to help or mentor someone else. I love God with all my heart, but I was not called to be a pastor. This doesn't mean I can't be a friend or even a mentor to someone in need. And the same is true for you.

Finally, get yourself a study Bible. Not just a Bible, but a study Bible. The Bible can be confusing. A study Bible will help you understand what you are reading. I'm gonna be honest with you here. I tried to read the Bible several times and wound up giving up because I felt like I was stupid since I didn't understand certain things. My study Bible helped me immensely. Any verse that you have questions about will be explained to you on the same page. It is really helpful, and I love to read the Bible now. Don't just read the Bible, study it. It's not a race. It's much better to read and study one verse a day and really understand it than to rush through a whole chapter just to say you read it, without getting anything out of it. Take your time and find someone to discuss this with if you would like. Most churches host a weekly Bible study group meeting, where they will dissect verses of the Bible each week.

This can be very helpful, but do this only if you're comfortable and when you feel ready. There is no pressure, and everything is at your pace. This is supposed to be exhilarating, not stressful. Remember, enjoy the process. This is the beginning of the rest of your life.

CHAPTER 12
LIFE'S WORTH LIVING

LIFE IS AMAZING. Regardless of how good it's been up to this point, it's about to get even better. If it hasn't been that great for you up to this point, that's about to change. Everything is better with God. Although life can be hard at times, it is an absolute gift. A gift that God wanted you to have. If someone takes the time, energy, and thought to present you with a gift, they would be very hurt if you hated it or discarded it. The same is true with God's gift of life. He didn't give you that gift for you to hate it, or to discard it, or even just to endure it. He presented it to you as a gift, and you should treat it that way. You are meant to love it and cherish it. It is meant to be enjoyed and used to bring joy to others. Treat every day as a blessing, because it is. Remember how many people didn't get that blessing today. Although we will all face many challenges in our lives, there are so many amazing things in life that outweigh the challenges. Before you had God in your life, your challenges may have appeared to be so big that you couldn't see the blessings. Now that you know how big your God is, you can probably barely see your challenges.

Each day will start out as good as you think it will, and it will progress into being as good as you make it! It's all about your attitude. Challenges are inevitable. It's not the challenges that slow you down; it's your attitude toward those challenges. You can let them break you, or you can let them make you. It's completely your choice. God is fighting your battles for you now, and there is no situation that is monumental to God. Instead of going into battle by yourself, you now have a partner, a tag-team partner. You can tag God in any time you want. He is always there, and He never gets tired—and He never loses. You never have to weather any storm alone anymore.

Life is short. Recognize that before it's too late. Look for the good in everything and everyone, and you will find it. Thank God every day for what you have, instead of complaining about what you have or don't have. There are people who have been given a lot and still complain. If that's the case, why would God give them more? Why would He give them more to complain about? On the other hand, there are people who hardly have anything but are grateful for all they do have. Live your life with gratitude. Use the whisper of time you have here to make the world a better place.

AN INVITATION FROM GOD

Ask God to fill you with His overwhelming godly peace —peace that can only be granted by Him. Be a blessing to others. Live your life with passion. Don't be another casualty of somebody who just existed but never lived. Life is too good to just survive. You are an absolute miracle, and you have so much to offer. It is my prayer that you understand that. There is nobody like you, and there never will be. Allow God to use you in ways you never thought possible. You can make a difference, even if it's just to one person. Your life is a life worth living. It's a life that only you can live. Live it to the fullest, because God loves you, and that's what He wants for you. Your future is a book of blank pages, and you are the author. How does your story end? Enjoy the journey!

AFTERWORD

I am so happy for you and the decisions you are making in your life. There is no bigger decision that you can ever make. It is my heartfelt prayer that this book will help you with your walk with God. You read my story. I didn't think that I would be the most likely candidate to have a close relationship with God. Thankfully, we are all candidates, and we get to nominate ourselves. If God can work in my life, I know He can work in yours. Just open up your heart to God and let Him in. You'll be amazed what He will do for you.

I would like to thank you from the bottom of my heart for allowing me to be even a small part of your new journey. I am completely humbled to be able to share some of my life with you. Welcome to your new beginning. Enjoy your new friendship with the Creator of the universe. I am so excited for you and where your

AFTERWORD

life is going. If it's all right to consider me your friend as well, I'd like to say I love you, and go do great things!

GOD BLESS YOU

ALSO BY STEVE JENNERICH

The Two Way Gift

NOTES

10. GOD'S NOT DONE WITH YOU

1. https://ourworldindata.org/grapher/number-of-deaths-per-year?time=1950..2018 A

Made in United States
Orlando, FL
03 December 2023